Home Cooking *with*
SAM&FOREST

ทำอาหารที่บ้านกับ แซม และ ฟอเรส

Home Cooking *with*
SAM&FOREST

ทำอาหารที่บ้านกับ แซม และ ฟอเรส

梁兆基
อรัญญา

 **Marshall Cavendish** Cuisine

Editor: Jolene Limuco
Designer: Bernard Go Kwang Meng
Photographer: Kiyoshi Yoshizawa, Jambu Studio

Copyright © 2011 Marshall Cavendish International (Asia) Private Limited

Published by Marshall Cavendish Cuisine
An imprint of Marshall Cavendish International
1 New Industrial Road, Singapore 536196

Other Marshall Cavendish Offices:
Marshall Cavendish International. PO Box 65829 London EC1P 1NY, UK • Marshall
Cavendish Corporation. 99 White Plains Road, Tarrytown NY 10591-9001, USA •
Marshall Cavendish International (Thailand) Co Ltd. 253 Asoke, 12th Flr, Sukhumvit
21 Road, Klongtoey Nua, Wattana, Bangkok 10110, Thailand • Marshall Cavendish
(Malaysia) Sdn Bhd, Times Subang, Lot 46, Subang Hi-Tech Industrial Park, Batu Tiga,
40000 Shah Alam, Selangor Darul Ehsan, Malaysia.

Marshall Cavendish is a trademark of Times Publishing Limited

National Library Board Singapore Cataloguing in Publication Data

Leong, Sam, 1966-
Home cooking with Sam & Forest. – Singapore : Marshall Cavendish Cuisine, c2011.
p. cm.
ISBN : 978-981-4346-56-6

1. Cooking, Chinese. 2. Cooking, Thai. 3. Quick and easy cooking. I. Leong, Forest,
1970- II. Title.

TX724.5.C5
641.5951 — dc22   OCN725597591

Printed in Singapore by KWF Printing Pte Ltd

目录
contents
สารบัญ

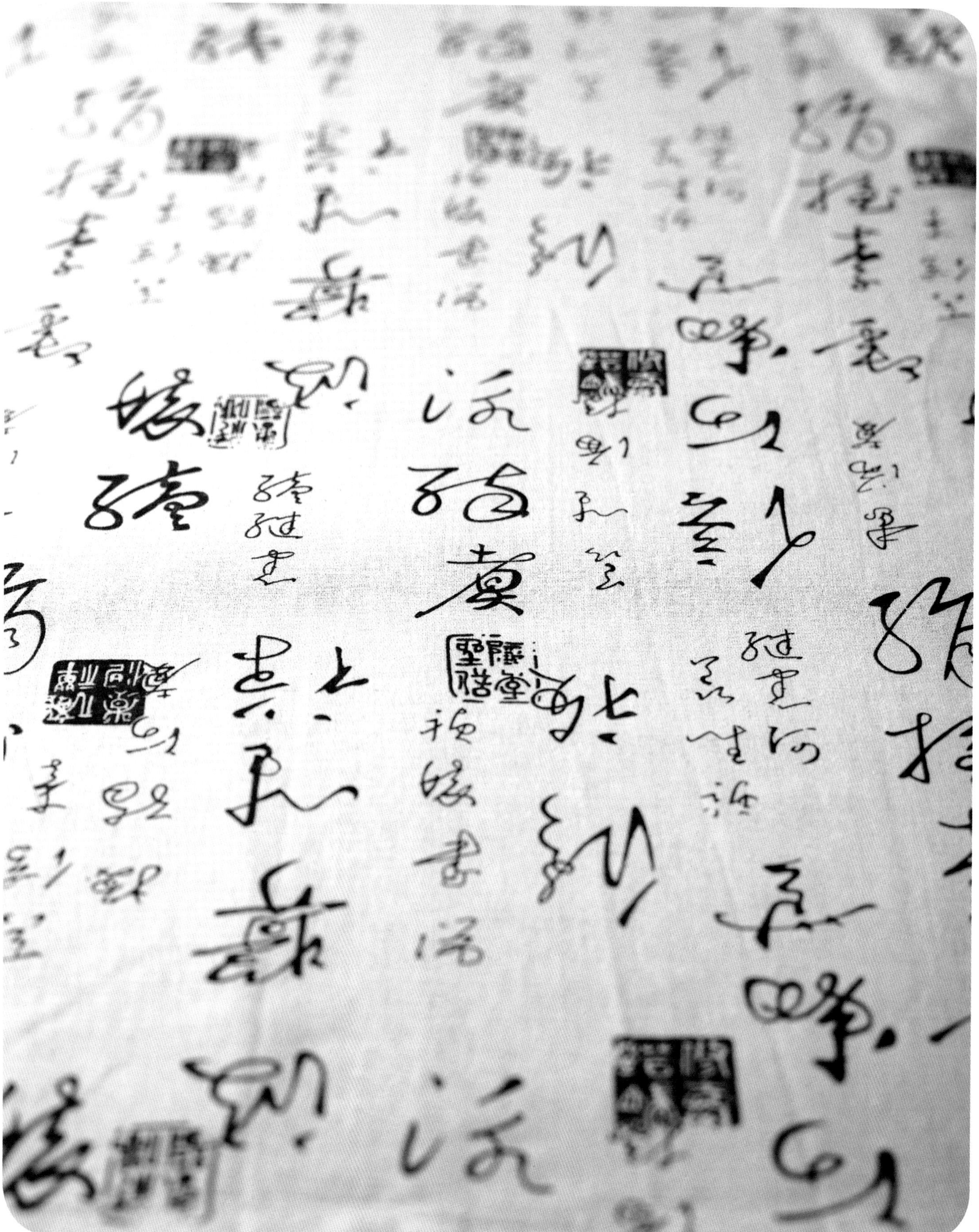

acknowledgements

致谢

คำขอบคุณ

We would like to thank Marshall Cavendish International (Asia) Pte Ltd for giving us the opportunity to publish this book, Yoshi-san for taking the beautiful photographs in this book; and Alan Chong, our first apprentice at the cooking school, for helping with the preparation of the dishes.

introduction

แนะนำเบื้องต้น

My father was a well-known chef in Malaysia and he was the one who inspired me to become a chef. When I became a successful chef, he advised me to go back to basics and share what I have learnt. Being a chef is hard work, and despite what you see on television and read in the newspapers, it is not all that glamorous.

Throughout my career as a chef in the past 27 years, I have been awarded many accolades, appeared on a few television shows, travelled all over the world and cooked for famous people. It was all very exciting. As a Chinese chef, I have fulfilled my dream. It is now time to share my knowledge and skills with people who are interested in cooking.

It was through my wife, Forest, also a chef by profession, that I developed an interest in culinary education. She is a cooking instructor at community centres and is very passionate about sharing her love and knowledge with home cooks. It was her dream to open her own cooking school and I realised that it was the perfect way for us to share our knowledge and skills in Chinese and Thai cooking. Thus, we opened Sam.Leong@Forest Cooking School.

Those who have attended my cooking classes know that although I have established myself as a modern Chinese chef at fine dining restaurants, I love nothing more than whipping up quick and simple meals at home. The collection of recipes in this book includes dishes that Forest and I enjoy making and sharing with our family and friends. We believe that home-cooked food is all about cooking what you feel comfortable with and what you enjoy eating. The recipes in this book are all very simple and easy to replicate in the home kitchen. They are perfect for novice cooks to learn how to cook Chinese dishes and Thai snacks. Those of you who are experienced cooks will find great ideas for delicious home-cooked meals. Use these recipes as a guide and omit or substitute ingredients and steps as you please. Just remember to enjoy yourself when cooking these dishes!

Sam Leong

One of my greatest joys is sharing my passion for cooking with others. My father, a retired chef, took the effort to share his cooking philosophy and skills with me early on. More than skills and techniques, he taught me about the joys of cooking, savouring and sharing meals with loved ones. This is one of the reasons why I started conducting cooking classes.

It was a dream come true when Sam and I opened our cooking school. Our goal is to provide hands-on culinary instruction and to share our love for home-cooked family meals.

Cooking is a rewarding process to be shared and enjoyed. The recipes in this book are some of our favourite, but most importantly, they are practical to make on a daily basis. Sam and I have combined our culinary knowledge to develop recipes that can be found at restaurants, yet are very easy to make at home. We want to make Chinese and Thai food accessible to all. We hope you enjoy cooking these dishes!

Forest Leong

汤羹

soups

แกง

Crabmeat and Bean Curd Broth 12 ·

Winter Melon Purée with Seafood Broth 14 ·

Double-boiled Shark's Fin Soup with
Chicken and Dried Scallops 16 ·

Simmered Duck Consommé with
Salted Vegetables 18 ·

Double-boiled Minced Pork Soup with
Water Chestnuts in Bamboo Cups 20 ·

Crabmeat and Bean Curd Broth

Serves 5

Chinese flowering cabbage (choy sum) 100 g (3¹/₂ oz), chopped

Vegetable oil 1 Tbsp

Chicken stock (see page 126) 1 litre (32 fl oz / 4 cups)

Salt 1 tsp

Sugar 1 tsp

Ground white pepper to taste

Chinese cooking wine (hua tiao) a dash

Crabmeat 250 g (9 oz)

Dried scallops (see page 126) 10

Silken bean curd 250 g (9 oz), cut into bite-size cubes

Corn flour (cornstarch) 1 Tbsp, mixed with 1 Tbsp water

Egg whites from 2 eggs

GARNISH

Wolfberries as desired

1. Boil a pot of water and poach Chinese flowering cabbage for 20 seconds. Plunge into a basin of cold water to stop cooking process. Drain well and set aside.

2. Heat oil in a wok and add chicken stock, salt, sugar, pepper and Chinese wine and bring to the boil.

3. Add crabmeat, scallops, bean curd and Chinese flowering cabbage. Adjust seasoning to taste. Stir in corn flour to thicken. Then add egg whites and stir until smooth.

4. Garnish with wolfberries and serve.

Winter Melon Purée with Seafood Broth Serves 5

Prawns (shrimps)
5, shelled and diced

Scallops *5, diced*

Winter melon *500 g (1 lb 1¹/₂ oz),
peeled and diced*

Vegetable oil *1 Tbsp*

Chicken stock (see page 126)
1 litre (32 fl oz / 4 cups)

Salt *1 tsp*

Sugar *1 tsp*

Ground white pepper *to taste*

Chinese cooking wine (*hua tiao*)
to taste

Dried scallops (see page 126) *5*

Corn flour (cornstarch) *1 Tbsp,
mixed with 1 Tbsp water*

MARINADE

Egg white *from 1 egg*

Salt *¹/₄ tsp*

Sugar *¹/₄ tsp*

Sesame oil *a dash*

Corn flour (cornstarch) *3 tsp*

GARNISH

Chopped spring onions (scallions)

1. Combine prawns, scallops and ingredients for marinade in a large bowl and mix well. Leave to marinate for at least 2 hours.

2. Bring a pot of water to the boil and lightly poach prawns and scallops, about 10 seconds. Drain well and set aside.

3. Bring a pot of water to the boil and poach winter melon for 30 minutes until soft. Remove and leave to cool. When cool, place cooked melon in a food processor and blend into a purée.

4. Heat oil in a wok and add chicken stock, salt, sugar, pepper and wine. Bring to the boil and add winter melon purée, dried scallops, prawns and scallops. Adjust seasoning to taste. Stir in corn flour to thicken.

5. Garnish with chopped spring onions.

Double-boiled Shark's Fin Consommé with Chicken and Dried Scallops Serves 4

Chicken drumsticks
5, deboned and skinned

Whole shark's fin *500 g
(1 lb 1¹/₂ oz)*

Dried scallops (see page 126) *5*

Chicken stock (see page 126)
1 litre (32 fl oz / 4 cups)

Salt *to taste*

Sugar *to taste*

Chinese cooking wine (*hua tiao*)
a dash

GARNISH
Coriander leaves (cilantro)

1. Bring a pot of water to the boil and poach chicken to remove impurities, about 30 seconds. Drain well.

2. Put chicken, shark's fin and dried scallops in a soup bowl.

3. Meanwhile, put chicken stock in a pot and bring to the boil. Season with salt, sugar and wine according to taste. Pour over ingredients in soup bowl and place in a steamer for 1 hour 30 minutes until chicken is soft and tender.

4. Garnish with coriander leaves and serve immediately.

NOTE You can prepare this dish in advance. After steaming, leave to cool at room temperature and keep refrigerated for up to 5 days. Re-heat before serving.

Simmered Duck Consommé with Salted Vegetables Serves 5

Duck ½, about 1 kg (2 lb 3 oz),
cut into pieces

Salted vegetables 15, *sliced and
soaked in water for 30 minutes*

Chicken stock (see page 126)
5 litres (160 fl oz / 20 cups)

Tomatoes 3, *large, diced*

Silken bean curd 250 g (9 oz),
cut into cubes

Salted plums 2

Ginger 2-cm (1-in),
peeled and sliced

Salt *to taste*

Sugar *to taste*

Ground white pepper *to taste*

Chinese cooking wine (*hua tiao*)
a dash

GARNISH
Spring onions (scallions)

1. Bring a pot of water to the boil and poach duck and salted vegetables to remove impurities, about 30 seconds. Drain and set aside.

2. Put all ingredients, except garnish, in a pot and bring to the boil over high heat. Boil for 30 minutes, then lower heat and simmer for 1 hour until liquid is reduced by half and duck is soft and tender.

3. Taste and adjust seasoning just before serving. Garnish with spring onions. Serve hot.

NOTE Be careful when seasoning the soup as the flavour will deepen after simmering for 1 hour 30 minutes. Only adjust seasoning to taste just before serving.

Double-boiled Minced Pork Soup with Water Chestnuts in Bamboo Cups Serves 10

Chicken stock (see page 126)
1.5 litres (48 fl oz / 6 cups)

Salt *2 tsp*

Sugar *1 tsp*

Ground white pepper *to taste*

Chinese cooking wine (*hua tiao*)
a dash

Dark soy sauce *a dash*

Minced pork *500 g (1 lb 1/2 oz)*

Water chestnuts *10, chopped*

Dried scallops (see page 126) *10*

Chopped coriander
(cilantro) stems *1 Tbsp*

GARNISH
Coriander leaves (cilantro)

1. Bring chicken stock to the boil and add salt, sugar, pepper, wine and dark soy sauce. Set aside to cool.

2. When soup is completely cool, add pork, water chestnuts, dried scallops and coriander stems and stir to mix well.

3. Divide soup into bamboo cups and place in a steamer for 3 hours or until pork is tender.

4. Garnish with coriander leaves and serve hot.

NOTE You can use heatproof small soup bowls if bamboo cups are unavailable.

fish & seafood

ปลา และ อาหาร ทะเล

Deep-fried Grouper with Sweet and
Sour Sauce 24 •

Steamed Sea Bass with Home-made
Soy Sauce 26 •

Steamed Cod Fillets with Pickled Red Chillies 28 •

Traditional Crab Dates (Cantonese-style Hoi Joe) 30 •

Steamed Crabs with Egg White and
Chinese Wine 32 •

Steamed Crabs with Pickled Red Chillies 34 •

My Lovely Black Pepper Crab 36 •

Stir-fried Tiger Prawns with
Black Pepper Sauce 38 •

Malaysian-style Stir-fried Tiger Prawns
with Oats 40 •

Stuffed Tempura Lychees 42 •

Deep-fried Prawns Wrapped in
Shredded Filo Pastry 44 •

Steamed Tiger Prawns with Minced Garlic in
Light Soy Sauce 46 •

Deep-fried Grouper with Sweet and Sour Sauce Serves 5

Grouper 1, about 800 g (1 ³/₄ oz)

Egg 1, beaten

Salt ¹/₄ tsp

Corn flour (cornstarch)
600 g (22 oz)

Canned diced pineapples
80 g (3 oz)

Red capsicum (bell pepper)
¹/₂, diced

Green capsicum (bell pepper)
¹/₂, diced

Tomato sauce
10 Tbsp + more to taste

SWEET AND SOUR SAUCE
Water 250 ml (8 fl oz / 1 cup)

Sugar 350 g (12 ¹/₂ oz)

Salt a pinch

Brown sugar 120 g (4 ¹/₂ oz)

White vinegar 150 ml (5 fl oz)

GARNISH
Coriander leaves (cilantro)

1. Prepare sweet and sour sauce. Combine all ingredients for sauce in a pan, except vinegar. Bring to the boil, stirring until sugar is dissolved. Leave to cool before stirring in vinegar.

2. Clean fish and butterfly it. Do this by inserting the tip of a very sharp knife into the belly of the fish near the tail. Slide the knife in until you feel the spine and slice along the length of the fish. Do not cut through the spine. Open the fish up, so it sits flat. Marinate fish with egg and salt for 10 minutes.

3. Heat oil for deep-frying. Coat marinated fish with corn flour and lower into hot oil. Deep-fry for 3 minutes until golden brown and crisp. Remove and drain well. Place on a serving dish.

4. Reheat 1 Tbsp oil in wok. Add capsicums and pineapple and stir-fry lightly. Add sweet and sour sauce and tomato sauce and bring to the boil.

5. Pour over fish, garnish with coriander leaves and serve immediately.

NOTE Add more tomato sauce if you want a thicker sauce.

Steamed Sea Bass with Home-made Soy Sauce Serves 5

Soy bean crumb 1

Corn oil 1 Tbsp

Sesame oil 1 Tbsp

Minced garlic 3 tsp

Chopped spring onions (scallions) 3 tsp

Salt to taste

Sugar 1 tsp

Hot bean sauce 1 tsp

Sea bass
1, about 800 g (1³/₄ oz), cleaned

SEASONING
Home-made soy sauce
(see page 128)
200 ml (6³/₄ fl oz)

GARNISH
Chilli oil

Chopped spring onions (scallions)

Red chillies as needed, seeded and chopped

1. Prepare soy bean crumb sauce. Soak soy bean crumb in water for 15 minutes. Remove from water, drain well and chop finely. Heat corn oil and sesame oil in a wok and sauté garlic and spring onions until fragrant. Add salt, sugar and hot bean sauce. Adjust seasoning to taste. Set aside.

2. Place chopsticks on a steaming plate and place sea bass on top. This will allow the sea bass to cook more evenly. Place in a steamer and steam for 10 minutes until cooked. To test if the fish is cooked, insert a chopstick into the thickest part of the fish. The chopstick should go through easily.

3. Top fish with prepared soy bean crumb sauce.

4. Spoon home-made soy sauce over fish.

5. Garnish with chilli oil, spring onions and chillies. Serve immediately.

Steamed Cod Fillets with Pickled Red Chillies Serves 5

Cod fillets
5, about 60 g (2 oz) each

Pickled red chillies (see page 129)
5 tsp

Home-made soy sauce
(see page 128)
200 ml (6³/₄ fl oz)

GARNISH

Chopped spring onions (scallions)

Crispy minced garlic
(see page 129)

1. Place fish fillets on a steaming plate and top fish with pickled red chillies. Place in a steamer and steam for 8 minutes or until fish is cooked. To test if fish is cooked, insert a chopstick into the fish. The chopstick should go through easily.

2. Spoon over home-made soy sauce.

3. Garnish with spring onions and garlic. Serve immediately.

NOTE For convenience, you can use bottled pickled chillies available from supermarkets for this dish.

Traditional Crab Dates
(Cantonese-style Hoi Joe) Serves 5

Crabmeat *200 g (7 oz)*

Chopped coriander
(cilantro) stems *50 g (2 oz)*

Water chestnuts
50 g (2 oz), chopped

Chopped coriander (cilantro)
25 g (1 oz)

Onion *1, big, peeled and
finely chopped*

Celery *1, finely chopped*

Carrot *1, peeled and finely chopped*

Crisp-fried shallots *50 g (2 oz)*

Egg *1, beaten*

Five spice powder *1/4 tsp*

Chicken seasoning *1/2 tsp*

Sugar *1 tsp*

Salt *1/2 tsp + more to taste*

Ground white pepper *a dash*

Chinese cooking wine (*hua tiao*)
a dash

Corn flour (cornstarch) *1 Tbsp*

Bean curd skin (unsalted) *1 sheet*

Cooking oil *for deep-frying*

GARNISH
Crispy lettuce
Sweet Thai chilli sauce

1. Combine all the ingredients, except bean curd skin and oil, in a large bowl and mix well.

2. Place mixture on bean curd skin and roll it up. Tie stuffed bean curd roll with string to form segments about the size of ping-pong balls. You will cut up the crab dates only after cooking.

3. Heat oil for deep-frying in a wok. Deep-fry the bean curd roll over medium heat until golden brown. Takes about 3 minutes. Drain. Remove the string and cut into segments.

4. Serve on crispy lettuce and a side of sweet Thai chilli sauce.

Steamed Crabs with Egg White and Chinese Wine Serves 5

Crabs 3, about 500 g
(1 lb 1¹/₂ oz) each

Ginger 5-cm (2-in) knob,
peeled and finely sliced

Chinese cooking wine (hua tiao)
a dash

SEASONING (COMBINED)

Egg white from 1 egg

Chicken stock (see page 126)
or water 4 Tbsp

Salt to taste

Sugar to taste

Sesame oil to taste

GARNISH

Coriander leaves (cilantro)

1. To kill crabs, place in the freezer for at least 2 hours. Pull off top shells and clean crabs. Chop into pieces, then rinse and drain well. Place crabs on a heatproof plate.

2. Pour ingredients for seasoning over crabs. Sprinkle ginger over and place in a steamer and steam for 10 minutes until crabs are cooked.

3. Pour Chinese wine over crabs. Garnish with coriander leaves and serve hot.

Steamed Crabs with Pickled Red Chillies Serves 5

Crabs *3, about 500 g (1 lb 1¹/₂ oz) each*

Crispy whole garlic (see page 130) *10*

SEASONING (COMBINED)

Pickled red chillies (see page 129) *5 tsp*

Corn flour (cornstarch) *1 Tbsp, mixed with 1 Tbsp water*

GARNISH

Chopped spring onions (scallions)

1. To kill crabs, place in the freezer for at least 2 hours. Pull off top shells and clean crabs. Chop into pieces, then rinse and drain well. Place crab on a heatproof plate.

2. Pour ingredients for seasoning over crabs. Sprinkle garlic over and place in a steamer to steam for 10 minutes until crabs are cooked.

3. Garnish with spring onions and serve hot.

NOTE For convenience, you can use bottled pickled chillies available from supermarkets for this dish.

My Lovely Black Pepper Crab

Serves 5

Crabs 3, *about 500 g*
(1 lb 1¹/₂ oz) each

Corn flour (cornstarch)
for coating crab before deep-frying

Unsalted butter *2 Tbsp*

Home-made black pepper sauce
(see page 127) *6 Tbsp*

Chopped spring onions (scallions)
2 Tbsp + more to garnish

Chinese cooking wine (*hua tiao*)
2 Tbsp

GARNISH

Crispy lettuce

1. To kill crabs, place in the freezer for at least 2 hours. Pull off top shells and clean crabs. Chop into pieces, then rinse and drain well.

2. Heat oil for deep-frying. Coat crabs with corn flour and lower into hot oil. Deep-fry for 2 minutes until golden brown. Remove and drain well.

3. Melt butter in a clean wok. Add crabs, black pepper sauce, spring onions and Chinese wine and toss to mix well.

4. Serve on crispy lettuce and garnish with more spring onions.

NOTE If you like a spicier dish, add freshly ground black pepper while sautéing the crabs with black pepper sauce.

Stir-fried Tiger Prawns with Black Pepper Sauce Serves 5

Prawns (shrimps) *10, large*

Egg white from *1 egg*

Salt *¼ tsp*

Sugar *¼ tsp*

Sesame oil *a dash*

Corn flour (cornstarch) *3 tsp, mixed with 3 tsp water + more to coat prawns for deep-frying*

Cooking oil *for deep-frying*

Unsalted butter *2 Tbsp*

Chopped spring onions (scallions) *2 Tbsp + more to garnish*

Home-made black pepper sauce (see page 127) *3 Tbsp*

Chinese cooking wine (*hua tiao*) *a dash*

GARNISH

Spring onions (scallions)

White sesame seeds

1. Prepare prawns. Peel prawns, then make a slit down the back of each one. Remove vein and rinse. Marinate with egg white, salt, sugar, sesame oil and corn flour mixture. Leave for at least 2 hours.

2. Heat oil for deep-frying. Coat prawns with corn flour and deep-fry for 1 minute until golden brown and crisp. Remove prawns and drain well.

3. Melt butter in a clean wok. Add prawns and stir-fry for a few seconds. Add black pepper sauce, spring onions and Chinese wine. Toss well to coat prawns with sauce.

4. Garnish with spring onions and white sesame seeds.

NOTE If you like a spicier dish, add freshly ground black pepper while sautéing the prawns.

Malaysian-style Stir-fried Tiger Prawns with Oats Serves 5

Tiger prawns (shrimps) *10, about 100 g (3¹/₂ oz) each*

Salt *¹/₂ tsp*

Sugar *¹/₂ tsp*

Cooking oil *for deep-frying*

Butter *2–3 Tbsp*

Instant oats *5 Tbsp*

Curry leaves *20*

Chopped pandan leaves *2 tsp*

Minced shallots *3 tsp*

Bird's eye chillies (*cili padi*) *2, seeded and finely chopped*

Salted egg yolks *from 3 eggs, cooked and finely minced*

1. Trim off prawn legs. Leave shells and tails on prawns. Cut prawns along the back and remove veins.

2. Season prawns with salt and sugar and leave to marinate for about 20 minutes.

3. Heat oil for deep-frying in a wok and cook prawns until just cooked. Drain well.

4. Heat butter in a clean wok. Add prawns and the remaining ingredients and stir-fry for a few minutes, making sure to toss the ingredients to coat prawns well.

5. Serve hot.

Stuffed Tempura Lychees Makes 10 pieces

Canned lychees *10, drained*

Crispy tempura flour
(see page 130) 80 g (3 oz)

Water *85 ml (2¹/₂ fl oz / ¹/₃ cup)*

Vegetable oil *2 Tbsp*

Cooking oil *for deep-frying*

Corn flour (cornstarch)
*for coating lychees
before deep-frying*

STUFFING

Unsalted butter *1 tsp*

Onion *¹/₂, peeled and
finely chopped*

Crabmeat *100 g (3¹/₂ oz)*

Chopped coriander
(cilantro) stems *50 g (2 oz)*

Corn flour (cornstarch) *1 Tbsp,
mixed with 1 Tbsp water*

SEASONING (COMBINED)

Chicken stock (see page 126)
4 Tbsp

Whipping cream *4 Tbsp*

Curry powder *¹/₂ tsp*

Salt *¹/₄ tsp*

Sugar *¹/₂ tsp*

1. Prepare stuffing. Heat butter in a wok and sauté onion until fragrant. Add seasoning ingredients, crabmeat and coriander stems and bring to boil. Stir in corn flour mixture to thicken. Remove and leave to cool.

2. Stuff mixture into lychees.

3. Combine crispy tempura flour, water and vegetable oil in a bowl and stir well.

4. Heat oil for deep-frying. Coat stuffed lychees with corn flour. Then coat with batter and lower in hot oil to cook until golden brown and crisp.

5. Serve hot.

Deep-fried Prawns Wrapped in Shredded Filo Pastry
Makes 10 pieces

Prawns (shrimps) *10, large*

Salted egg yolks from
*10 salted eggs, boiled in water for
2 minutes and shelled*

Canned smoked oysters
10, brine reserved for marinade

Store-bought shredded filo pastry
3–4 sheets

Cooking oil *for deep-frying*

MARINADE

Egg *1, beaten*

Salt *1/4 tsp*

Sugar *1/4 tsp*

Sesame oil *1/4 tsp*

Chinese cooking wine (*hua tiao*)
a dash

Corn flour (cornstarch) *1 Tbsp*

1. Prepare prawns. Peel prawns, then make a slit down the back of each one. Remove vein and rinse. Marinate with egg, smoked oyster brine, salt, sugar, sesame oil, wine and corn flour for at least 30 minutes.

2. Place a salted egg yolk and oyster on top of each prawn and roll it up, then repeat to wrap with shredded filo pastry.

3. Place prawns in a preheated oven at 120°C (250°F) and cook for 2 minutes until pastry is crisp.

4. Heat oil for deep-frying and cook baked parcels for 1 minute until golden brown. Drain well.

5. Serve hot.

NOTE Baking the prawns rolls in the oven will prevent them from coming apart when deep-frying.

Steamed Tiger Prawns with Minced Garlic in Light Soy Sauce

Serves 5

Tiger prawns (shrimps)
10, about 100 g (3¹/₂ oz) each

Garlic *10 cloves, peeled and finely minced*

Salt *¹/₄ tsp*

Sugar *¹/₄ tsp*

Sesame oil *a dash*

Chinese cooking wine (hua tiao) *a dash*

Corn flour (cornstarch) *1 Tbsp*

Cooking oil *2 Tbsp*

SEASONING

Home-made soy sauce (see page 128) *100 ml (3¹/₃ fl oz)*

GARNISH

Chopped spring onions (scallions)

Coriander leaves (cilantro)

1. Trim off prawn legs. Leave shells and tails on prawns. Cut prawns halfway lengthwise, then arrange on a steaming plate.

2. Combine garlic, salt, sugar, sesame oil, wine, corn flour and cooking oil in a bowl and pour over prawns. Place in a steamer and steam for 4 minutes until prawns are cooked.

3. Pour home-made soy sauce over prawns. Garnish with spring onions and coriander leaves.

肉类 家禽

meat & poultry

เนื้อ, เป็ด และ ไก่

Minced Pork Belly Wrapped in
Bean Curd Skin 50 •

Crispy Dough Fritters Stuffed with
Minced Pork 52 •

Champagne Pork Ribs 54 •

Crispy Pork Ribs Marinated in
Fermented Bean Curd 56 •

Stir-fried Chicken with Black Pepper Sauce 58 •

Steamed Herbal Chicken 60 •

Traditional Salt-baked Chicken 62 •

Deep-fried Chicken Wings Marinated in
Fermented Prawn Paste 64 •

Crispy Lemon Chicken 66 •

Kung Pao Chicken with Cashew Nuts 68 •

Stir-fried Chicken with Basil 70 •

Chicken Cooked with Wine, Ginger and
Wood Ear Fungus 72 •

Stir-fried Roasted Minced Duck Meat with
Pine Nuts on Crispy Lettuce 74 •

Braised Duck with Ginger 76 •

Steamed Chawanmushi with Century Egg and
Salted Egg Yolk 78 •

Minced Pork Belly Wrapped in Bean Curd Skin Serves 5

Bean curd skin (unsalted)
*5 sheets, cut into 15 x 15-cm
(6 x 6-in) squares*

Cooking oil *for deep-frying + 2 Tbsp*

Minced garlic *1 Tbsp*

Shiitake mushrooms *4–5,
finely chopped and poached*

Corn flour (cornstarch) *1 Tbsp,
mixed with 1 Tbsp water*

STUFFING

Minced pork belly *200 g (7 oz)*

Chopped coriander (cilantro) stems
1 Tbsp

Water chestnuts *4–5, chopped*

Egg *1, beaten*

Salt *$^1/_2$ tsp*

Sugar *$^1/_2$ tsp*

Chinese cooking wine (*hua tiao*)
a dash

Corn flour (cornstarch) *1 tsp*

SEASONING (COMBINED)

Chicken stock (see page 126)
400 ml (13$^1/_2$ fl oz)

Fermented soy bean paste
(*tau cheo*) *$^1/_2$ tsp*

Oyster sauce *$^1/_2$ tsp*

Sugar *$^1/_4$ tsp*

Sesame oil *1 Tbsp*

Dark soy sauce *a dash*

Chinese cooking wine (*hua tiao*)
a dash

GARNISH

Chopped spring onions (scallions)

1. Combine ingredients for stuffing in a large bowl and mix well.

2. Place stuffing on bean curd skins and roll stuffing up to form parcels.

3. Heat cooking oil for deep-frying and cook stuffed bean curd rolls until golden brown and crisp. Drain well and set aside.

4. Heat 2 Tbsp oil in a clean wok and sauté garlic and mushrooms until fragrant. Add ingredients for seasoning and stuffed bean curd rolls and simmer for 2 minutes. Stir in corn flour mixture to thicken sauce.

5. Garnish with spring onions and serve hot.

Crispy Dough Fritters Stuffed with Minced Pork Makes about 10

Minced pork belly *300 g (11 oz)*

Chopped coriander (cilantro) stems *1 Tbsp*

Celery *1/2 stalk, finely chopped*

Water chestnuts *3–4, finely chopped*

Egg *1, beaten*

Sugar *1/2 tsp*

Salt *1/2 tsp*

Light soy sauce *2 tsp*

Five spice powder *1/4 tsp*

Chinese cooking wine (*hua tiao*) *a dash*

Sesame oil *1–2 tsp*

Corn flour (cornstarch) *2 Tbsp*

Deep-fried crullers (*you tiao*) *2*

Cooking oil *for deep-frying*

Mayonnaise

1. Combine all the ingredients, except deep-fried crullers, oil and mayonnaise, in a large bowl and mix well to form a paste.

2. Cut deep-fried crullers into bite-size pieces and stuff with pork mixture.

3. Heat oil for deep-frying and cook stuffed deep-fried crullers over medium heat until brown and crisp.

4. Serve with mayonnaise on the side.

NOTE Try to buy deep-fried crullers that are not too dark in colour as you will cook it again.

Champagne Pork Ribs Serves 5

Pork ribs (soft bone)
600 g (1 lb 5¹/₃ oz)

Ginger 5-cm (1-in) knob,
peeled and sliced

Spring onion (scallion) *1*

Coriander (cilantro) *1 sprig*

Leek *1, cleaned and finely sliced*

Red chilli *1, seeded and finely sliced*

Garlic *5 cloves, peeled and
finely chopped*

Chicken stock (see page 126) or
water *1 litre (32 fl oz / 4 cups)*

Oyster sauce *1 tsp*

Fermented soy bean paste
(*tau cheo*) *1 tsp*

Sugar *1 tsp*

Chinese cooking wine (*hua tiao*)
1 Tbsp

Dark soy sauce *1 Tbsp*

Cooking oil
for deep-frying + ¹/₂ Tbsp

Corn flour (cornstarch) *for coating
pork ribs before deep-frying*

CHAMPAGNE SAUCE
Lemon-lime soda
250 ml (8 fl oz / 1 cup)

Champagne
180 ml (6 fl oz / ³/₄ cup)

Freshly squeezed lemon juice
80 ml (2¹/₂ fl oz / ¹/₃ cup)

Salt *¹/₄ tsp*

GARNISH
Crispy lettuce

White sesame seeds

1. Bring a pot water to the boil and poach pork ribs to remove impurities, about 20 seconds. Drain.

2. Put pork ribs in a pot and add enough water to cover. Add the remaining ingredients, except cooking oil and corn flour. Simmer over low heat for 1 hour or until pork ribs are tender. Remove ribs and discard contents of pot.

3. Heat oil for deep-frying. Coat ribs with corn flour and deep-fry until brown and crisp. Remove and drain well.

4. Prepare champagne sauce. Combine all ingredients for sauce in a saucepan and bring to the boil. Remove and set aside.

5. Heat ¹/₂ Tbsp oil in a wok. Add pork ribs and champagne sauce and toss well.

6. Serve on crispy lettuce and garnish with white sesame seeds.

Crispy Pork Ribs Marinated in Fermented Bean Curd Serves 5

Pork ribs (soft bone)
600 g (1 lb 5 1/3 oz)

Egg 1, beaten

Fermented bean curd (fu yu)
40 g (1 1/2 oz)

Sugar 1 Tbsp

Chinese cooking wine (hua tiao)
3 Tbsp

Mui Kui Loo wine or vodka 3 Tbsp

Baking soda 1/4 tsp

Ground white pepper to taste

Chopped coriander
(cilantro) stems 1 Tbsp

Chopped shallots 1 Tbsp

Chopped garlic 1 Tbsp

Potato flour 50 g (2 oz)

Cooking oil for deep-frying

Corn flour (cornstarch) for coating
pork ribs before deep-frying

GARNISH
Crispy lettuce

1. Combine all ingredients, except oil and corn flour, in a large bowl and leave to marinate for at least 6 hours.

2. Heat oil for deep-frying in a wok. Coat pork ribs in corn flour and deep-fry until golden brown and crisp. Remove and drain well.

3. Serve on crispy lettuce.

Stir-fried Chicken with Black Pepper Sauce Serves 5

Chicken drumsticks
3, deboned and diced

Cooking oil *for deep-frying +
2 Tbsp*

Spring onions (scallions)
2, chopped

Young ginger *5-cm (2-in) knob,
finely minced*

Home-made black pepper sauce
(see page 127) *3 Tbsp*

Chinese cooking wine (*hua tiao*)
a dash

Corn flour (cornstarch)
1 Tbsp, mixed with 1 Tbsp water

MARINADE

Egg *1*

Oyster sauce *2 Tbsp*

Light soy sauce *1 tsp*

Sugar *¹/₄ tsp*

Chinese cooking wine (*hua tiao*)
2 tsp

Corn flour (cornstarch) *1 tsp*

1. Combine chicken and ingredients for marinade in a large bowl and mix well. Leave to marinate for at least 2 hours.

2. Heat oil for deep-frying. Deep-fry chicken over medium heat until golden brown and crisp. Remove and drain well.

3. Heat 2 Tbsp oil in a wok and stir-fry spring onions and ginger until fragrant. Add chicken, black pepper sauce and wine and continue to stir-fry for a few minutes. Stir in corn flour mixture to thicken sauce.

4. Garnish as desired and serve.

Steamed Herbal Chicken Serves 5

Whole spring chicken
1, about 500 g (1 lb 1/2 oz)

Angelica roots (*dang gui*)
2, cleaned

Wolfberries
20, soaked in water to soften

Polygonatum (*yoke chok*)
10, cleaned

Codonopsis polisula (*dang shen*)
2, cleaned

Chinese dates *5*

Coriander (cilantro) stems *5 stalks*

Corn flour (cornstarch) *1 Tbsp,*
mixed with 1 Tbsp water

SEASONING (COMBINED)
Chicken stock (see page 126)
500 ml (16 fl oz / 2 cups)

Salt *1 tsp*

Sugar *1 tsp*

Chinese cooking wine (*hua tiao*)
a dash

GARNISH
Coriander leaves (cilantro)

1. Bring a pot of water to the boil. Add chicken and poach very briefly to cook lightly, about 20 seconds. Drain well.

2. Place the remaining ingredients in a big heatproof bowl and place the chicken on top.

3. Place seasoning ingredients in a pot and bring to the boil. Stir in corn flour to thicken.

4. Pour seasoning over chicken and place in a steamer to steam over boiling water for 2 hours until chicken is cooked and tender. Garnish with coriander leaves.

Traditional Salt-baked Chicken

Serves 5

Chicken drumsticks 5, *deboned*

Cooking oil 2 *Tbsp*

Angelica roots (*dang gui*)
5, *cleaned*

Wolfberries 2 *Tbsp*

Coriander (cilantro) stems 5 *stalks*

MARINADE

Egg 1

Oyster sauce 3 *tsp*

Salt 3 *tsp*

Sugar 2 *tsp*

Minced ginger 2 *tsp*

Minced coriander (cilantro) stems
2 *tsp*

Dark soy sauce *a dash*

Chinese cooking wine (*hua tiao*)
a dash

Corn flour (cornstarch) *a dash*

1. Combine chicken and ingredients for marinade in a large bowl and mix well. Leave to marinate for at least 2 hours.

2. Heat oil in a pan and brown chicken on both sides.
Do not cook chicken.

3. On a piece of aluminium foil, place angelica roots, wolfberries, coriander stems and chicken and fold the aluminium foil to seal ingredients. Cook in a preheated oven at 220°C (425°F) for 12–15 minutes.

Deep-fried Chicken Wings Marinated in Fermented Prawn Paste Serves 5

Chicken wings (mid-joints)
1 kg (2 lb 3 oz)

Cooking oil *for deep-frying*

MARINADE

Fermented prawn (shrimp) paste
(*ha cheong*) 40 g (1 1/2 oz)

Sugar 1 *Tbsp*

Chinese cooking wine (*hua tiao*)
3 *Tbsp*

Egg 1

Potato flour 1 *Tbsp*

Corn flour (cornstarch)
50 g (2 oz)

Freshly ground black pepper
to taste

GARNISH

Crispy lettuce

Bottled chilli sauce (optional)

1. Combine chicken and ingredients for marinade in a large bowl and mix well. Leave to marinate for at least 4 hours.

2. Heat oil for deep-frying and cook chicken until golden brown and crisp. Drain well.

3. Serve on crispy lettuce with a side of chilli sauce, if desired.

Crispy Lemon Chicken Serves 5

Chicken drumsticks
2, deboned and skinned

Cooking oil *for deep-frying +*
¹/₂ Tbsp

Corn flour (cornstarch) *for coating*
chicken before deep-frying

MARINADE

Egg *1*

Salt *¹/₄ tsp*

Sugar *¹/₄ tsp*

Five spice powder *¹/₄ tsp*

Chinese cooking wine (*hua tiao*)
a dash

LEMON SAUCE

Lemon juice concentrate
250 ml (8 fl oz / 1 cup)

Water *350 ml (11²/₃ fl oz)*

Freshly-squeezed lemon juice
from 2 lemons

Sugar *100 g (3¹/₂ oz)*

Salt *¹/₂ tsp*

Corn flour (cornstarch)
1 Tbsp, mixed with 1 Tbsp
custard powder and 1 Tbsp water

GARNISH

Lemon slices

White sesame seeds

Coriander leaves (cilantro)

1. Combine chicken and ingredients for marinade in a large bowl and mix well. Leave to marinate for at least 2 hours.

2. Heat oil for deep-frying. Coat chicken with corn flour and deep-fry until golden brown and crisp. Remove and drain well. Leave to cool, then slice chicken into bite-size pieces.

3. Prepare lemon sauce. Combine lemon juice concentrate, water, fresh lemon juice, sugar and salt in a pot and bring to the boil, stirring constantly until sugar dissolves.

4. Heat ¹/₂ Tbsp oil in a wok. Add lemon sauce and bring to the boil. Stir in corn flour mixture to thicken sauce.

5. Pour sauce over chicken and garnish with lemon, sesame seeds and coriander leaves.

NOTE   The addition of custard powder in the corn flour mixture gives the sauce a lovely yellow tinge.

Kung Pao Chicken with Cashew Nuts Serves 5

Chicken drumsticks
4, deboned and skinned

Cooking oil *for deep-frying +*
¹/₂ Tbsp

Dried chillies *50 g (2 oz), soaked in
water to soften, seeded and sliced*

Spring onions (scallions)
100 g (3¹/₂ oz)

Crispy whole garlic (see page 130)
50 g (2 oz)

Home-made Kung Pao sauce
(see page 127) *250 ml
(8 fl oz / 1 cup)*

Corn flour (cornstarch)
1 Tbsp, mixed with 1 Tbsp water

MARINADE

Egg *1*

Salt *¹/₄ tsp*

Sugar *¹/₄ tsp*

Five-spice powder *¹/₄ tsp*

Chinese cooking wine (*hua tiao*)
a dash

GARNISH

Cashew nuts

1. Combine chicken and ingredients for marinade in a large bowl and mix well. Leave to marinate for at least 2 hours.

2. Heat oil for deep-frying and cook chicken over medium heat until brown and crisp. Remove and drain well.

3. Heat ¹/₂ Tbsp oil in a wok. Add dried chillies and fry until fragrant. Then add spring onions, garlic and chicken. Stir well and add Kung Pao sauce. Stir in corn flour mixture to thicken sauce.

4. Garnish with cashew nuts and serve.

Stir-fried Chicken with Basil Serves 5

Chicken drumsticks
4, deboned and skinned

Cooking oil
for deep-frying + 1/2 Tbsp

Crispy whole garlic
(see page 130) *10*

Crispy whole shallots
(see page 130) *10*

Spring onions (scallions) *2, cut into
3 x 3-cm (1 1/2 x 1 1/2-in) lengths*

Ginger *5-cm (2-in) knob,
peeled and sliced*

Red chillies *3, seeded and sliced*

Basil leaves *10*

MARINADE

Egg *1*

Salt *1/4 tsp*

Sugar *1/4 tsp*

Five-spice powder *1/4 tsp*

Chinese cooking wine (*hua tiao*)
a dash

SAUCE

Chinese rice wine *2 Tbsp*

Chinese cooking wine (*hua tiao*)
2 Tbsp

Light soy sauce *2 Tbsp*

Hot bean sauce *1 Tbsp*

Black vinegar *1 Tbsp*

Rock sugar *2 Tbsp*

Honey *1 Tbsp*

Dark soy sauce *100 ml (3 1/3 fl oz)*

Corn flour (cornstarch)
1 Tbsp, mixed with 1 Tbsp water

1. Combine chicken and ingredients for marinade in a large bowl and mix well. Leave to marinate for at least 2 hours.

2. Heat cooking oil for deep-frying and cook chicken until golden brown and crisp. Remove and drain well.

3. Combine ingredients for sauce, except corn flour, in a pot and bring to the boil.

4. Heat 1/2 Tbsp oil in a clean wok and stir-fry garlic, shallots, spring onions, ginger and chillies until fragrant.

5. Add chicken and sauce. Stir in corn flour mixture to thicken. Add basil and mix well. Serve.

Chicken Cooked with Wine, Ginger and Wood Ear Fungus

Serves 5

Chicken drumsticks
3, deboned, skinned and diced

Cooking oil *2 Tbsp*

Ginger *1-cm (¹/₂-in) knob,
peeled and finely sliced*

Eggs *2, beaten*

Wood ear fungus *2–3, shredded
and soaked in hot water to soften*

Angelica roots (*dang gui*)
4, cleaned

Wolfberries *2 Tbsp,
soaked in water to soften*

Chicken stock (see page 126)
500 ml (16 fl oz / 2 cups)

Salt *¹/₂ tsp*

Sugar *¹/₂ tsp*

Sesame oil *a dash*

Chinese cooking wine (*hua tiao*)
a dash

MARINADE

Egg *1*

Oyster sauce *2 tsp*

Light soy sauce *1 tsp*

Sugar *¹/₄ tsp*

Chinese cooking wine (*hua tiao*)
2 tsp

Corn flour (cornstarch) *1 tsp*

GARNISH

Chopped spring onions (scallions)

1. Combine chicken and ingredients for marinade in a large bowl and mix well. Leave to marinate for at least 2 hours.

2. Bring a pot of water to the boil and briefly poach chicken to remove impurities. Drain and set aside.

3. Heat oil in a wok and sauté ginger until fragrant. Add eggs and sauté for a while. Then add chicken and the remaining ingredients. Bring to the boil over high heat. Boil for a few minutes until stock is cloudy. Adjust seasoning to taste.

4. Garnish with spring onions and serve.

Stir-fried Roasted Minced Duck Meat with Pine Nuts on Crispy Lettuce Serves 10

Shiitake mushrooms
10, cleaned and chopped

Celery *2 stalks, chopped*

Chopped carrots *3 Tbsp*

Cooking oil *for shallow-frying*

Minced garlic *1 tsp*

Minced shallots *1 tsp*

Water chestnuts
10, peeled and chopped

Chopped coriander
(cilantro) stems *3 Tbsp*

Cooked roast duck
*¹/₂, about 1 kg (2 lb 3 oz),
deboned and finely diced*

Corn flour (cornstarch)
1 Tbsp, mixed with 1 Tbsp water

SEASONING (COMBINED)

Chicken stock (see page 126)
5 Tbsp

Oyster sauce *1 Tbsp*

Light soy sauce *¹/₂ Tbsp*

Sugar *¹/₂ Tbsp*

Chinese cooking wine (*hua tiao*)
a dash

Sesame oil *a dash*

Dark soy sauce *a dash*

GARNISH

Crispy lettuce

Pine nuts

1. Bring a pot of water to the boil. Add mushrooms, celery and carrots and poach very briefly to cook. Drain well and set a side.

2. Heat oil for shallow-frying in a wok and stir-fry garlic and shallots until fragrant.

3. Add the mushrooms, celery, carrots, water chestnuts, coriander stems and roast duck and stir-fry for a few minutes.

4. Add seasoning ingredients and stir-fry for a few more minutes. Stir in corn flour mixture to thicken.

5. Spoon over lettuce leaves and garnish with pine nuts. Serve immediately.

Braised Duck with Ginger Serves 5

Duck ¹/₂, about 1 kg (2 lb 3 oz), chopped into pieces

Cooking oil for shallow-frying

Chopped ginger 300 g (11 oz)

Fermented soy bean bean paste (tau cheo) 1 tsp

Chinese dates 10

Cinnamon 1 stick

Star anise 2

Chicken stock (see page 126) 2 litres (64 fl oz / 8 cups)

Oyster sauce 1 tsp

Sugar ¹/₂ tsp

Chinese cooking wine (hua tiao) a dash

Dark soy sauce a dash

Corn flour (cornstarch) 1 Tbsp, mixed with 1 Tbsp water

GARNISH

Crispy whole garlic (see page 130) 10, sliced

Chopped spring onions (scallions)

Wolfberries as needed, soaked in water to soften

1. Bring a pot of water to the boil and briefly poach duck to remove impurities. Drain and set aside.

2. Heat oil in a wok and stir-fry ginger and fermented soy bean paste until fragrant. Add the remaining ingredients, except corn flour and garnish, and continue to stir-fry for about 2 minutes.

3. Add duck and simmer over low heat for about 1 hour 30 minutes until duck is tender. Stir in corn flour mixture to thicken sauce.

4. Garnish with garlic, spring onions and wolfberries. Serve hot.

Steamed Chawanmushi with Century Egg and Salted Egg Yolk
Makes about 10 cups

Eggs 6, *beaten*

Water *900 ml (30³/₄ fl oz)*

Salt *¹/₄ tsp*

Hon-dashi powder (instant dashi) *3 tsp*

Light soy sauce *5 tsp*

Mirin *¹/₂ tsp*

Sake *¹/₂ tsp*

Century egg *1, diced*

Salted egg yolks *2, diced*

GARNISH
Coriander leaves (cilantro)

1. Combine ingredients, except century egg and salted egg yolks, in a bowl and mix well. Using a sieve, strain mixture to remove any lumps.

2. Divide mixture into small heatproof soup bowls or teacups. Place bowls or teacups in a steamer and steam for 20 minutes or until *chawanmushi* is set.

3. Once set, arrange century egg and salted egg yolks on top and return *chawanmushi* to the steamer for another 5 minutes.

4. Garnish with coriander leaves and serve immediately.

蔬菜 豆腐
vegetables &
bean curd
ผัก และ เต้าหู้

Poached Spinach with Three Eggs 82 ·

Poached Chinese Cabbage with
Dried Scallops 84 ·

Steamed Bean Curd Topped with Scallops
and XO Sauce 86 ·

Crispy Bean Curd with Dipping Sauce 88 ·

Deep-fried Bean Curd Stuffed with
Minced Prawns (Traditional Pipa Tofu) 90 ·

Poached Spinach with Three Eggs Serves 4

Spinach *400 g (14 oz)*

Cooking oil *2 Tbsp*

Chicken stock (see page 126)
400 ml (13 1/2 fl oz)

Chinese cooking wine (*hua tiao*)
a dash

Salt *1/4 tsp*

Sugar *1/4 tsp*

Ground white pepper *a dash*

Century egg *1, diced*

Salted egg yolk *1, diced*

Dried scallops (see page 126)
2, shredded

Corn flour (cornstarch)
1 Tbsp, mixed with 1 Tbsp water

Egg *1, beaten*

1. Bring a pot of water to the boil and blanch spinach with a drop of oil for about 4 minutes until soft. Drain and place spinach on a plate.

2. Heat oil in a wok and add chicken stock, wine, salt, sugar and pepper. Bring to the boil and add century egg, salted egg yolk and dried scallops. Stir in corn flour to thicken, then stir in egg.

3. Pour sauce over spinach and serve hot.

NOTE To prevent raw salted egg yolk from sticking to your knife and chopping board, coat salted egg yolk and knife with a little oil before cutting.

Poached Chinese Cabbage with Dried Scallops Serves 5

Chinese cabbage (stems only)
*500 g (1 lb 1 1/2 oz),
cut into 5-cm (2-in) squares*

Salt *to taste*

Cooking oil *1 Tbsp*

Dried scallops (see page 126)
10, shredded

Corn flour (cornstarch)
1 Tbsp, mixed with 1 Tbsp water

SEASONING (COMBINED)
Chicken stock (see page 126)
250 ml (8 fl oz / 1 cup)

Oyster sauce *1 Tbsp*

Sugar *1/2 tsp*

Sesame oil *1 tsp*

Dark soy sauce *1 tsp*

Chinese cooking wine (*hua tiao*)
1 tsp

GARNISH
Chopped spring onions (scallions)

1. Bring a pot of water to the boil and add cabbage. Season with a pinch of salt and boil for about 15 minutes or until cabbage is soft. Drain and place on a serving plate.

2. Heat oil in a wok and add ingredients for seasoning. Bring to the boil, then add dried scallops. Adjust seasoning to taste. Stir in corn flour to thicken. Pour sauce over cabbage.

3. Garnish with spring onions and serve.

Steamed Bean Curd Topped with Scallops and XO Sauce *Serves 6*

Scallops *12, finely chopped*

Water chestnuts
6, peeled and chopped

Chopped coriander stems
(cilantro) *1 Tbsp*

Silken bean curd 2 tubes, about
*250 g (9 oz) each, cut into
12 rounds*

Corn flour (cornstarch)
for dusting bean curd

SEASONING (COMBINED)

Salt *¼ tsp*

Sugar *¼ tsp*

Sesame oil *a dash*

Corn flour (cornstarch) *3 tsp*

Egg white from *1 egg*

GARNISH

Home-made XO sauce
(see page 128)

Chopped spring onions (scallions)

1. Combine scallops, water chestnuts, coriander stems and ingredients for seasoning in a bowl and mix well. Set aside.

2. Using a melon baller, scoop out a bit of the top of each bean curd round. Dust each bean curd round with a bit of corn flour. Place bean curd in a steamer and steam for 2 minutes to get rid of excess water.

3. Using a teaspoon, shape the scallop mixture into balls and place on bean curd rounds. Top with home-made XO sauce and steam for 4 minutes or until scallop mixture is cooked.

4. Garnish with spring onions and serve.

Crispy Bean Curd with Dipping Sauce Serves 5

Silken bean curd *3 blocks, about 250 g (9 oz) each*

Salt *a pinch*

Cooking oil *for deep-frying*

DIPPING SAUCE

Tomato sauce *1 Tbsp*

Dark soy sauce *2 Tbsp*

Freshly-squeezed lime juice *1/2 Tbsp*

GARNISH

Crispy lettuce

1. Start preparations a day ahead. Place bean curd on a tray and cover with a bit of water. Sprinkle over with some salt and leave to soak for 30 minutes.

2. Remove bean curd from water and place on a steamer and steam for 15 minutes. Set aside and leave to cool to room temperature. Transfer to a refrigerator to keep overnight.

3. Cut bean curd into bite-size squares.

4. Heat oil for deep-frying in a wok over very high heat and cook bean curd until golden brown and crisp.

5. Prepare dipping sauce. Combine ingredients for dipping sauce in a bowl and mix well. Set aside.

6. Serve bean curd on crispy lettuce with dipping sauce on the side.

NOTE Use a perforated plate with a hole when steaming the bean curd so any excess water will be drained off. This will ensure that the bean curd is crisp after deep-frying.

Deep-fried Bean Curd Stuffed with Minced Prawns (Traditional Pipa Tofu)

Serves 5

Prawns (shrimps) *10, medium*

Chopped coriander stems
(cilantro) *1 Tbsp*

Water chestnuts
2–3, peeled and finely chopped

Carrot *1/3, peeled and
finely chopped*

Silken bean curd
*1 tube, about 250 g (9 oz),
cut into rounds*

Cooking oil *2 Tbsp +
more for deep-frying*

Corn flour (cornstarch) *for coating
bean curd before deep-frying*

SEASONING (COMBINED)
Egg white from *1 egg*

Salt *1/2 tsp*

Sugar *1/2 tsp*

Ground white pepper *a dash*

Sesame oil *a dash*

Corn flour (cornstarch) *4 tsp*

GARNISH
Crispy lettuce

1. Peel and devein prawns. Rinse, then finely chop prawns. Mix prawns with coriander stems, water chestnuts, carrot and ingredients for seasoning.

2. Coat a soup spoon with a bit of oil and scoop up some prawn mixture. Shape into an oval and brush with a bit of egg white. Repeat until prawn mixture is used up.

3. Place bean curd pieces in a steamer and steam for 5 minutes. Remove.

4. Heat oil for deep-frying. Coat steamed bean curd pieces with some corn flour and deep-fry until golden brown and crisp.

5. Serve on crispy lettuce.

米面饭类

rice & noodles

ข้าวและบะหมี่

Rice Cooked in Chicken Consommé with Seafood 94 ·

Fried Rice with Crabmeat and Prawn Roe 96 ·

Rice with Braised Pork (Lu Rou Fan) 98 ·

Rice with Bean Curd in Hot Bean Sauce (Mapo Tofu) 100 ·

Malaysian-style Crispy Egg Noodles with Tiger Prawns 102 ·

Stir-fried Mouse-tail Noodles with Minced Pork Belly in Black Pepper Sauce 104 ·

Rice Cooked in Chicken Consommé with Seafood Serves 5

Scallops *4, diced*

Prawns (shrimps)
4, cleaned, shelled and diced

Cooking oil *for shallow-frying*

Chicken stock (see page 126)
500 ml (16 fl oz / 2 cups)

Cooked long-grain rice *200 g (7 oz)*

Salt *a dash*

Sugar *a dash*

Sesame oil *a dash*

Chinese cooking wine (*hua tiao*)
a dash

Crabmeat *100 g (3¹/₂ oz)*

Chinese flowering cabbage
(*choy sum*) *100 g (3¹/₂ oz),
chopped and poached*

Chopped coriander
(cilantro) stems *2 tsp*

MARINADE
Egg white from *1 egg*

Salt *¹/₄ tsp*

Sugar *¹/₄ tsp*

Sesame oil *a dash*

Corn flour (cornstarch) *3 tsp*

GARNISH
Crisp-fried shallots

1. Combine scallops, prawns and ingredients for marinade in a bowl and mix well. Leave to marinate for at least 2 hours.

2. Bring a pot of water to the boil and briefly poach scallops and prawns for about 20 seconds. Drain and set aside.

3. Heat oil in a wok and add chicken stock and rice. Bring to the boil and season to taste with salt, sugar, sesame oil and Chinese wine.

4. Add prawns, scallops, crabmeat, Chinese flowering cabbage and coriander stems. Simmer for 5 minutes until rice is soft.

5. Garnish with crisp-fried shallots and serve immediately.

NOTE If you like this dish to be more soupy, increase the amount of chicken stock used.

Fried Rice with Crabmeat and Prawn Roe Serves 5

Cooking oil *2 Tbsp*

Eggs *3, beaten*

Crabmeat *100 g (3¹/₂ oz)*

Carrot *¹/₃, medium, peeled, diced and poached*

Chinese flowering cabbage *(choy sum) 50 g (2 oz), chopped*

Cooked long-grain rice *500 g (1 lb 1¹/₂ oz)*

Prawn (shrimp) roe *(ebiko) 4 Tbsp*

SEASONING (COMBINED)

Salt *¹/₂ tsp*

Sugar *¹/₂ tsp*

Ground white pepper *a dash*

1. Heat oil in a wok and add eggs. When eggs are starting to set, scramble them, then add crabmeat, carrot, Chinese flowering cabbage and rice. Stir-fry until fragrant.

2. Add ingredients for seasoning and stir-fry until rice is fragrant once again.

3. Dish out and stir in prawn roe until well mixed. Serve immediately.

NOTE If you want every grain of rice to be coated with egg very lightly and add the rice even before the eggs start to set.

Rice with Braised Pork (Lu Rou Fan)

Serves 10

Pork belly *1 kg (2 lb 3 oz)*

Cooking oil *2 Tbsp*

Garlic *5 cloves,*
peeled and finely chopped

Shallots 5, *peeled and finely chopped*

Red chillies
2, seeded and finely sliced

Fermented bean curd (*fu yu*)
2 pieces

Star anise *1*

Cinnamon *1 stick*

Cloves *2*

Chicken stock (see page 126)
enough to cover pork belly

Black bean soy sauce
3 Tbsp

Rock sugar *40 g (1 1/2 oz)*

Corn flour (cornstarch)
1 Tbsp, mixed with 1 Tbsp water

Freshly-cooked long-grain rice
500 g (1 b 1 1/2 oz)

Chopped spring onions (scallions)

1. Bring a pot of water to the boil and briefly poach pork belly to remove impurities, about 20 seconds. Plunge into a basin of iced water and drain well. Leave to cool and cut into small cubes.

2. Heat oil in a wok and add garlic, shallots and chillies and stir-fry until fragrant. Add pork and fermented bean curd and continue to stir-fry until fragrant. Add the remaining ingredients, except corn flour, and bring to the boil. Simmer for 45 minutes over low heat, adding more chicken stock if mixture becomes too dry. Stir in corn flour mixture to thicken sauce.

3. Scoop hot cooked rice into serving bowls and spoon pork mixture over. Garnish with spring onions and serve immediately.

Rice with Bean Curd in Hot Bean Sauce (Mapo Tofu) Serves 10

Silken bean curd *2 blocks, about 250 g (9 oz) each, diced*

Cooking oil *2 Tbsp*

Minced garlic *1/2 tsp*

Minced shallots *1/2 tsp*

Crabmeat *100 g (3 1/2 oz)*

Shiitake mushrooms *5, finely chopped and poached*

Corn flour (cornstarch) *1 Tbsp, mixed with 1 Tbsp water*

Freshly-cooked long-grain rice *500 g (1 b 1 1/2 oz)*

SEASONING (COMBINED)

Chicken stock (see page 126) *200 ml (6 fl oz / 3/4 cup)*

Bottled mapo tofu sauce or hot bean sauce *1 tsp*

Oyster sauce *1 tsp*

Sugar *1/2 tsp*

Dark soy sauce *a dash*

Sesame oil *a dash*

GARNISH

Chopped spring onions (scallions)

Chilli oil (optional)

1. Place bean curd pieces in a bowl of hot water and stir in a few drops of dark soy sauce. Set aside for 10 minutes. This will give the bean curd some colour.

2. Heat oil in a wok and stir-fry garlic and shallots until fragrant. Add mushrooms and the ingredients for seasoning and bring to the boil. Adjust seasoning to taste. Stir in corn flour to thicken sauce.

3. Add bean curd and stir gently.

4. Scoop bean curd mixture over rice and garnish with spring onions and chilli oil, if desired.

Malaysian-style Crispy Egg Noodles with Tiger Prawns Serves 5

Prawns (shrimps)
10, cleaned and shelled

Egg noodles *2 bundles, about 400 g (14 oz)*

Cooking oil
4 Tbsp + more if needed

Garlic *2 cloves, peeled and finely minced*

Ginger *5-cm (2-in) knob, peeled and finely sliced*

Carrot *1/2, peeled, sliced and poached*

Corn flour (cornstarch) *1 Tbsp, mixed with 1 Tbsp water*

Egg *1, beaten*

Chinese flowering cabbage
(*choy sum*) *as desired, poached*

MARINADE

Egg white from *1 egg*

Salt *1/4 tsp*

Sugar *1/4 tsp*

Sesame oil *a dash*

Corn flour (cornstarch) *3 tsp*

SEASONING (COMBINED)

Chicken stock (see page 126)
400 ml (13 1/2 fl oz)

Salt *a dash*

Oyster sauce *a dash*

Sugar *a dash*

Ground white pepper *a dash*

Chinese cooking wine
(*hua tiao*) *a dash*

1. Combine prawns and ingredients for marinade in a large bowl and mix well. Leave to marinate for at least 2 hours.

2. Bring a pot of water to the boil and briefly poach egg noodles for 20 seconds. Plunge into a basin of cold water and drain well.

3. Heat 2 Tbsp oil in a wok and spread noodles out in wok. Gently sear noodles until crispy on one side. Turn noodles over and sear other side. Add more oil if needed. Drain and place noodles on a serving plate.

4. Heat 2 Tbsp oil in a clean wok and stir-fry garlic and ginger until fragrant. Add prawns, carrot and seasoning ingredients. Bring to the boil and adjust seasoning to taste. Stir in corn flour mixture to thicken sauce.

5. Turn off the heat. Pour egg into the wok and stir gently.

6. Pour sauce over noodles and top with Chinese flowering cabbage.

Stir-fried Mouse-tail Noodle with Minced Pork Belly in Black Pepper Sauce Serves 5

Mouse-tail noodles (*loh shee fun*) 500 g (1 lb 1 1/2 oz)

Minced pork belly 250 g (9 oz)

Cooking oil 2 Tbsp

Eggs 3, *beaten*

Bean sprouts 200 g (7 oz)

Spring onions (scallions) 2, *chopped*

Onion 1, *large, peeled and finely chopped*

Red chillies 2, *seeded and finely sliced*

SEASONING (COMBINED)

Home-made black pepper sauce (see page 127) 1 Tbsp

Oyster sauce 1 Tbsp

Worcestershire sauce 1/2 Tbsp

Sugar 1/2 tbsp

Sesame oil *a dash*

Ground white pepper *a dash*

Dark soy sauce *a dash*

GARNISH

Chopped spring onions (scallions)

Toasted white sesame seed

1. Bring a pot of water to the boil and briefly poach noodles and minced pork belly separately for 10 seconds each. Drain and set aside.

2. Heat oil in a wok and add eggs. When eggs are starting to set, scramble them, then add noodles and pork and stir-fry for a few more minutes.

3. Add in the remaining ingredients and ingredients for seasoning and stir-fry until fragrant.

4. Garnish with spring onions and white sesame seeds. Serve immediately.

NOTE Dark soy sauce adds colour to this dish. Adjust the amount added to your preference. For convenience, you can use bottled black pepper sauce available from supermarkets.

甜点

desserts
ของหวาน

Steamed Green Tea Cupcakes

Makes 20 cupcakes

Cake flour 260 g (9 oz)

Baking powder 1 Tbsp

Green tea powder 2 Tbsp

Eggs 2

Castor sugar 220 g (8 oz)

Sponge cake stabiliser (Ovalette) 3/4 Tbsp

Evaporated milk 125 ml (4 fl oz / 1/2 cup)

Lime juice 1 tsp

Water 150 ml (4 fl oz / 1/2 cup)

Vanilla extract 1/2 tsp

Green food colouring (optional) a few drops

1. Sift cake flour, baking powder and green tea powder together in a large bowl.

2. In a separate bowl, beat eggs, sugar and sponge cake stabliser until light and fluffy.

3. Add evaporated milk, lime juice, half the water and vanilla and beat until smooth.

4. Add flour mixture and the remaining water. Mix well and add colouring, if using.

5. Spoon the mixture into small cupcake liners and steam over low to medium heat for 15–20 minutes.

Easy Steamed Milk Custard with Ginger Juice Makes 4–5 cups

Castor sugar *110 g (4 oz)*

Milk *500 ml (16 fl oz / 2 cups)*

Egg whites from
5 large eggs, lightly beaten

Ginger juice *2–3 Tbsp, extracted
from 2.5-cm (1-in) knob ginger*

1. Combine milk and sugar in a bowl and stir until sugar dissolves. Gently fold in egg whites.

2. Add ginger juice and strain the mixture with a sieve.

3. Divide the mixture among 4–5 small heatproof teacups or bowls. Place in a steamer and steam for 30–40 minutes or until custard is set. Garnish as desired and serve warm or chilled.

Bananas in Syrup Serves 5

Coconut cream *150 ml (5 fl oz)*

Salt *¹/₄ tsp*

Sugar *400 g (14 oz)*

Water *200 ml (7 fl oz)*

Small bananas (half-ripe)
*10–20, peeled and soaked in
water and 1 Tbsp lime juice for
at least 2 hours*

1. Prepare sauce. Mix coconut cream with salt and boil over medium heat for about 5 minutes. Remove from heat and set aside.

2. Boil sugar and water over high heat until sugar dissolves. When syrup starts to thicken, reduce heat to low.

3. Drain the bananas and add to the syrup. Cook, stirring occasionally, until bananas start to become translucent, about 10–15 minutes.

4. Drain bananas from syrup and top with coconut sauce. Serve immediately.

NOTE When stirring the bananas, do so gently to avoid breaking up the bananas.

Baked Tapioca Cake (Ba Bin) Serves 5–8

Water *125 ml (4 fl oz / ¹/₂ cup)*

Palm sugar *(gula Melaka)*
200 g (7 oz)

Castor sugar *170 g (6 oz)*

Tapioca *300–400 g
(10¹/₂–14oz / 3–4 cups), grated*

Skinned grated coconut
90 g (3 oz)

Coconut cream
300 ml (10 fl oz / 1¹/₄ cups)

1. Boil water, palm sugar and castor sugar in a saucepan over low heat. Once sugar dissolves, remove from heat and set aside to cool.

2. Combine tapioca, grated coconut and coconut cream in a bowl and add sugar syrup and stir well to combine.

3. Preheat oven to 190°C–200°C (375°F–400°F).

4. Lightly grease a 20 × 20-cm (8 × 8-in) baking tray or line with baking paper. Pour in the mixture and bake for 20 minutes. Increase the temperature to 230°C (450°F) and bake for another 5 minutes or until top of cake is browned. Remove from heat and leave to cool before cutting into bite-size pieces.

Thai Layer Cake Serves 6–8

Coconut cream
1 litre (32 fl oz / 4 cups)

Castor sugar *450 g (1 lb)*

Arrow root or green bean flour
200 g (7 oz)

Rice flour *120 g (4½ oz)*

Tapioca flour *200 g (7 oz)*

Pandan extract (optional)
a few drops

Purple food colouring
a few drops

1. Warm coconut cream in a saucepan and then add sugar. Stir until sugar dissolves and set aside to cool.

2. Combine the three kinds of flour in a mixing bowl. Add cooked coconut cream a little at a time and stir the mixture until smooth. Add pandan extract, if using.

3. Separate the flour mixture into 2 portions. Add food colouring to each portion.

4. Prepare a 20 x 20-cm (8 x 8-in) tray for steaming by heating it up over a pot of boiling water for about 5 minutes.

5. Measure about 160 ml (5½ fl oz) of one mixture and pour into the tray. Steam over high heat for 5 minutes.

6. Measure the same amount of coloured mixture and pour into the tray. Steam over high heat for 5 minutes.

7. Repeat the process of layering until the mixtures are used up. There will be about 9–10 layers. When the final layer is poured in, steam for 10 minutes. Remove from heat and leave to cool before cutting into bite-size pieces.

Sweet Sago with Creamy Durian

Serves 5–6

Water *1.5 litres (48 fl oz / 6 cups)*

Small sago pearls *200 g (7 oz)*

Sugar *100 g (3½ oz)*

DURIAN CREAM

Water *3 Tbsp*

Green bean flour *1 Tbsp*

Coconut milk *125 ml (4 fl oz / ½ cup)*

Salt *½ tsp*

Ripe durian flesh *from 1 medium durian*

GARNISH

Young coconut flesh

Black sesame seeds

1. Boil a large pot of water and add sago pearls. Cook for about 10 minutes or until sago is transluscent. Stir well to prevent sago from clumping together. Once sago thickens, reduce heat.

2. Add sugar and cook for another 2–3 minutes. Remove from heat and set aside.

3. Meanwhile, prepare durian cream. Combine water and green bean flour in a medium bowl and stir well to combine.

4. Boil coconut milk in a pot. Add salt and green bean flour mixture and cook until mixture starts to thicken.

5. Add durian flesh and cook for another 2–3 minutes.

6. To serve, spoon sago into serving cups and top with durian cream and garnish with coconut flesh and sesame seeds, if desired.

Osmanthus Jelly Serves 5

Water *1.5 litres (48 fl oz / 6 cups)*

Osmanthus blossoms
10 g (1/3 oz)

Konnyaku jelly powder
15 g (1/2 oz)

Castor sugar *220 g (8 oz)*

Chinese wolfberries (optional)
10 g (1/3 oz)

Canned fruit cocktail (optional)
as needed

1. Boil water in a pot and add osmanthus blossoms and continue to boil for 10–15 minutes.

2. Meanwhile, mix jelly powder with sugar and add to the pot. Stir well. When jelly powder completely dissolves, remove from heat. Stir in the wolfberries.

3. Divide mixture into moulds and allow it to cool in the refrigerator for 1 hour or until set.

4. Remove jelly from moulds and serve with fruit cocktail, if desired.

Pandan Dumplings in Coconut Cream Serves 4–5

Pandan leaves 5–6, chopped

Water *180 ml (6 fl oz / ³/₄ cup)*

Glutinous rice flour
180 g (6¹/₄ oz)

White sesame seeds

SAUCE

Coconut cream
250 ml (8 fl oz / 1 cup)

Salt *1 tsp*

Sugar *100 g (3¹/₂ oz)*

Water or coconut juice
250 ml (8 fl oz / 1 cup)

Young coconut flesh
100 g (3¹/₂ oz)

1. Combine pandan leaves with 180 ml (6 fl oz / ³/₄ cup) water in a food processor and blend well. Strain and measure out 125 ml (4 fl oz / ¹/₂ cup) pandan juice.

2. To make dumplings, slowly pour pandan juice into glutinous rice flour and mix well to form a smooth paste.

3. Roll mixture into small balls about 1-cm (¹/₂-in) in diameter.

4. Boil a large pot of water and cook glutinous rice balls. They are cooked when they float to the surface.

5. Prepare sauce. Combine coconut cream, salt, sugar and water or coconut juice in a saucepan and bring to the boil. Add coconut flesh and simmer for about 3–5 minutes.

6. Serve pandan dumplings with coconut cream in individual bowls. Garnish with sesame seeds, if desired.

基本食谱
basic recipes
สูตรพื้นฐาน

The following recipes are for stocks, sauces and condiments that are used frequently in Chinese cooking.

Once you are familiar with the taste and flavours of these basic stocks, sauces and condiments, you can use them to perk up other recipes.

Chicken Stock Makes about 3 litres (96 fl oz / 12 cups)

Chicken stock can be prepared ahead of time and kept refrigerated for up to 3 days or frozen for up to 1 month. Alternatively, ready-made chicken stock packed into cartons can be purchased from most supermarkets. If using ready-made chicken stock, look for those without added seasoning.

Water *5 litres (160 fl oz / 20 cups)*

Chicken *1, about 1 kg (2 lb 3 oz)*

Chicken feet *1 kg (2 lb 3 oz)*

Lean pork *1 kg (2 lb 3 oz)*

Chinese (*Yunnan*) ham *350 g (12 oz)*

1. Bring water to the boil in a pot and add chicken, chicken feet, lean pork and ham. Simmer over low heat for 5 hours, or until about 3 litres (96 fl oz / 12 cups) stock is left in the pot.

2. Strain stock before using.

Steamed Dried Scallops Prepares 20 scallops

Like home-made chicken stock, steamed dried scallops take time to prepare, so cook up a large batch and keep refrigerated for up to 1 week.

Dried scallops *20, medium*

Chicken stock (see above) *as needed*

Salt *1/4 tsp*

Ginger *2 slices*

Spring onion (scallion) *1, chopped*

Cooking oil *1 tsp*

1. Soak dried scallops in water and leave for 2 hours.

2. Drain dried scallops and put into a steaming bowl. Add enough chicken stock to cover scallops, then add salt, ginger, spring onion and cooking oil. Put into a steamer and steam for 45 minutes.

3. Use the dried scallops together with the liquid.

Home-made Black Pepper Sauce

Makes about 400 ml (13^1/$_2$ fl oz)

Prepare this in advance and keep refrigerated for up to 1 week. Ready-made black pepper sauce is also available at most supermarkets.

Water 160 ml (5 fl oz)

Maggi seasoning sauce 2 Tbsp

Freshly ground black pepper 35 g (1 oz)

Tomato sauce 300 ml (10 fl oz / 1^1/$_4$ cups)

Brown (steak) sauce 2 Tbsp

Sugar 50 g (2 oz)

Unsalted butter 80 g (3 oz), melted

1. Combine all ingredients for sauce in a pot. Bring to the boil, stirring until sugar is dissolved.

2. Use as needed.

Home-made Kung Pao Sauce

Makes about 400 ml (13^1/$_2$ fl oz)

This can be prepared ahead of time and kept refrigerated for up to 1 week. Ready-made *kung pao* sauce can be purchased from most supermarkets.

Black vinegar 1 bottle, about 300 ml (10 fl oz / 1^1/$_4$ cups)

Bottled chilli sauce 125 ml (4 fl oz / 1^1/$_2$ cup)

Sugar 125 g (4^1/$_2$ oz)

Oyster sauce 4 Tbsp

Maggi seasoning sauce 100 ml (3^1/$_3$ fl oz)

Dark soy sauce 4 Tbsp

Chicken stock (see page 126) 125 ml (4 fl oz / 1^1/$_2$ cup)

Chinese cooking wine (*hua tiao*) a dash

Star anise powder a dash

Black vinegar a dash

1. Combine all the ingredients, except black vinegar, in a pot. Bring to the boil, stirring until sugar is dissolved.

2. Leave to cool before stirring in black vinegar.

3. Use as needed.

Home-made Soy Sauce
Makes about 100 ml (3¹/₃ fl oz)

Although similar in appearance to light soy sauce, this home-made soy sauce is highly fragrant due to the use of ginger, spring onion and coriander. Make up a large batch and keep it in a clean jar for use whenever you need it.

Cooking oil ¹/₂ Tbsp

Ginger 2 slices

Spring onion (scallion) 1, cut into short lengths

Coriander leaves (cilantro) 2 sprigs

Chicken stock (see page 126) 320 ml (10 fl oz)

Light soy sauce 70 ml (2¹/₃ fl oz)

Dark soy sauce a dash

Rock sugar 45 g (1¹/₂ oz)

1. Heat oil in a wok and stir-fry ginger, spring onion and coriander until fragrant. Add remaining ingredients and bring to the boil.

2. Strain and use as needed.

Home-made XO Sauce
Makes about 100 g (3¹/₂ oz)

XO sauce will add a distinctive spicy flavour to dishes. Make sure there is enough oil to cover the XO sauce. For more flavour, you can add more dried scallops. This can be stored in a clean airtight container in the refrigerator for up to 1 month.

Cooking oil for shallow-frying

Dried prawns (shrimps) 100 g (3¹/₂ oz), washed and finely minced

Garlic 3 heads, peeled and finely minced

Shallots 5, peeled and finely minced

Bird's eye chillies (cili padi) 5, seeded and finely minced + 8, seeded and diced

Dried scallops 20, soaked to soften and shredded

Chicken seasoning ¹/₂ Tbsp

Sugar 2 Tbsp

Salt 1 Tbsp

Store-bought dried prawn (shrimp) powder 1 Tbsp

1. Heat oil in a wok and stir-fry dried prawns over medium heat until crispy and fragrant. Drain well and set aside.

2. Reheat oil in the wok and stir-fry garlic and shallots until fragrant. Add fried dried prawns and the remaining ingredients. Stir-fry the ingredients over low heat for 10 minutes.

3. Use as needed.

Pickled Red Chillies
Makes about 500 ml (16 fl oz / 2 cups)

Pickled red chilli is available in jars from some supermarkets. If unavailable, you can make your own using this recipe. Pickled red chillies can be stored in a clean container in the refrigerator indefinitely.

Red chillies *400 g (14 1/2 oz), stalks removed*

White vinegar *80 ml (2 1/2 fl oz / 1/3 cup)*

Salt *2 Tbsp*

Ginger *4 slices*

1. Start preparations a week ahead.

2. Chop chillies finely. Do not use a blender or the chillies will not keep. Transfer to a plastic bottle with a screw cap and add vinegar, salt and ginger. Leave at room temperature for 7 days. This will rid chillies of their spiciness.

3. Use as needed.

Crispy Minced Garlic
Makes about 3 Tbsp

Crispy minced garlic will keep in a clean airtight container for up to 1 week.

Garlic *3 heads, peeled*

Cooking oil *for deep-frying*

1. Mince garlic and rinse, then place in a strainer to drain well.

2. Heat oil for deep-frying over medium heat. Add minced garlic and cook in batches for about 2 minutes until garlic is brown and crisp. Remove and drain well.

3. Use as needed.

Crispy Whole Garlic/Shallots

Prepares 3 heads of garlic or 10 shallots

Garlic *3 heads, peeled or
10 shallots, peeled*

Cooking oil *for deep-frying*

1. Rinse garlic/shallots and place in a strainer to drain well.

2. Heat oil for deep-frying over medium heat. Add garlic/shallots and cook in batches for about 2 minutes until brown and crisp. Remove and drain well.

3. Use as needed.

Tempura Flour
Makes about 2 kg (4 lb 6 oz)

Wheat flour *1.5 kg (3 lb 4^1/$_2$ oz)*

Glutinous rice flour *150 g (5^1/$_3$ oz)*

Pure potato flour *150 g (5^1/$_3$ oz)*

Baking powder *120 g (4^1/$_2$ oz)*

Baking soda *30 g (1 oz)*

1. Combine ingredients in a bowl and mix well.

2. Use as needed.

食材

glossary

ภาคผนวก

AMERICAN GINSENG

Also known as *yang shen* (Chinese) or *yong sam* (Cantonese), ginseng is believed to invigorate the body and encourage healing after illness. There are many grades of ginseng, so feel free to exercise your options of using a grade of ginseng that suits your budget.

ANGLED LUFFA

Angled luffas belong to the melon family. They have stiff longitudinal ridges and are typically 30–60-cm (12–24-in) in length. Select dark green and thin melons, as these tend to be younger. Older melons may sometimes be bitter.

DRIED SCALLOPS

Also known as *conpoy*, these dried sea scallops are available in various sizes and vary in quality. They have a strong flavour and are usually added to steamed or stewed dishes. Dried scallops will keep indefinitely if stored in a clean airtight container in a cool, dry place.

FERMENTED BEAN CURD (FU YU)

Also known as preserved bean curd or bean curd cheese, fermented bean curd is aged in brine and flavoured with chilli. It has a pungent flavour and a dense but smooth and creamy texture, not unlike soft cheese. It can be eaten as is with porridge, or used as a condiment or flavouring. Fermented bean curd is sold in jars.

FERMENTED SOY BEAN PASTE

Also known as yellow or brown bean paste, this salty condiment is sold in jars, with the beans whole or mashed. The whole beans can be mashed for greater flavour when cooking. Keep the paste refrigerated after opening and it will keep indefinitely.

OSMANTHUS BLOSSOMS

Also known as *gui hua* (Chinese), these small dried yellow flowers have a light floral fragrance and are typically used to flavour teas or Chinese desserts, and sometimes used as a garnish. Osmanthus blossoms can be purchased from Chinese herbal stores.

PICKLED RED CHILLIES

These are minced red chillies preserved in vinegar. The vinegar removes the hotness of the chillies, leaving just a mouthwatering tangy flavour, making it ideal for seasoning bland foods like fish.

SHREDDED FILO PASTRY

Although not commonly used in Chinese cooking, shredded filo pastry is used like breadcrumbs to coat food with a crisp outer layer. Shredded filo pastry is popularly used in Greek and Middle Eastern cooking; where it is used to make desserts. Bake pastry in a preheated oven at 120°C (250°F) for 2 minutes before deep-frying to keep it from coming apart when cooking. You can find shredded filo pastry in the frozen section of most supermarkets.

SOY BEAN CRUMB

Known better by its Chinese name, *dou so*, this is a product from Taiwan. It is made from soy beans that are dry-roasted and chopped, then compressed into a ball. It is available from the dry goods store in some markets.

WOOD EAR FUNGUS

Also known as black fungus, black fungus is sold dried and must be reconstituted by soaking in water. Once softened, cut away any hard woody bits and discard. Although bland with no taste of its own, wood ear fungus is enjoyed for its crunchy texture. It is typically sliced and added to stir-fries, soups or stews.

weights & measures

น้ำหนัก ชั่ง และ ตวง

Quantities for this book are given in Metric, Imperial and American (spoon) measures.
Standard spoon and cup measurements used are: 1 tsp = 5 ml, 1 Tbsp = 15 ml, 1 cup = 250 ml.
All measures are level unless otherwise stated.

LIQUID AND VOLUME MEASURES

Metric	Imperial	American
5 ml	1/6 fl oz	1 teaspoon
10 ml	1/3 fl oz	1 dessertspoon
15 ml	1/2 fl oz	1 tablespoon
60 ml	2 fl oz	1/4 cup (4 tablespoons)
85 ml	2 1/2 fl oz	1/3 cup
90 ml	3 fl oz	3/8 cup (6 tablespoons)
125 ml	4 fl oz	1/2 cup
180 ml	6 fl oz	3/4 cup
250 ml	8 fl oz	1 cup
300 ml	10 fl oz (1/2 pint)	1 1/4 cups
375 ml	12 fl oz	1 1/2 cups
435 ml	14 fl oz	1 3/4 cups
500 ml	16 fl oz	2 cups
625 ml	20 fl oz (1 pint)	2 1/2 cups
750 ml	24 fl oz (1 1/5 pints)	3 cups
1 litre	32 fl oz (1 3/5 pints)	4 cups
1.25 litres	40 fl oz (2 pints)	5 cups
1.5 litres	48 fl oz (2 2/5 pints)	6 cups
2.5 litres	80 fl oz (4 pints)	10 cups

DRY MEASURES

Metric	Imperial
30 grams	1 ounce
45 grams	1 1/2 ounces
55 grams	2 ounces
70 grams	2 1/2 ounces
85 grams	3 ounces
100 grams	3 1/2 ounces
110 grams	4 ounces
125 grams	4 1/2 ounces
140 grams	5 ounces
280 grams	10 ounces
450 grams	16 ounces (1 pound)
500 grams	1 pound, 1 1/2 ounces
700 grams	1 1/2 pounds
800 grams	1 3/4 pounds
1 kilogram	2 pounds, 3 ounces
1.5 kilograms	3 pounds, 4 1/2 ounces
2 kilograms	4 pounds, 6 ounces

OVEN TEMPERATURE

	°C	°F	Gas Regulo
Very slow	120	250	1
Slow	150	300	2
Moderately slow	160	325	3
Moderate	180	350	4
Moderately hot	190/200	370/400	5/6
Hot	210/220	410/440	6/7
Very hot	230	450	8
Super hot	250/290	475/550	9/10

LENGTH

Metric	Imperial
0.5 cm	1/4 inch
1 cm	1/2 inch
1.5 cm	3/4 inch
2.5 cm	1 inch